Doncaster
Metropolitan Borough Council

DONCASTER LIBRARY AND INFORMATION SERVICES
www.doncaster.gov.uk

Please return/renew this item by the
last date shown.
Thank you for using your library.

InPress 0231 June 09

The Greeks

ROSEMARY REES

Heinemann

First published in Great Britain by
Heinemann Library
an imprint of Heinemann Publishers
(Oxford) Ltd
Halley Court, Jordan Hill, Oxford OX2 8EJ

OXFORD LONDON EDINBURGH MADRID
ATHENS BOLOGNA PARIS MELBOURNE
SYDNEY AUCKLAND SINGAPORE TOKYO
IBADAN NAIROBI HARARE GABORONE
PORTSMOUTH NH (USA)

98 97 96 95 94
10 9 8 7 6 5 4 3 2 1

**British Library Cataloguing in Publication
Data is available from the British Library
on request.**

ISBN 0 431 07802 5 (hardback)
      0 431 07783 5 (paperback)

Designed by Ron Kamen, Green Door
Design Ltd, Basingstoke

Printed in China

Photographic acknowledgements
The author and publishers wish to
acknowledge with thanks the following
photographic sources:

a = above b = below l = left r = right

Agora Excavations 1970, American School
of Classical Studies at Athens p40b; Ancient
Art and Architecture Collection pp7a and b,
11a and b, 16a, 17, 19b, 20a and b, 21c and
b, 22, 27, 32a, 36, 37b, 46a and b, 56b;
Bridgeman Art Library pp9 and cover, 58; C
M Dixon pp4a, 6, 8, 13a, 21b and b, 23, 31a,
32b, 45b, 50b and cover; Ekdotike Athenon
pp 19a, 24, 25a, 34a and title page, 49, 55a
and b; Robert Harding Photographic
Library pp26, 38a, 43; Hirmer Fotoarchiv
p31b; Michael Holford pp4b, 10, 12, 13b,
15a and b; Kunsthistorisches Museum,
Vienna pp56a, Mansell Collection pp14,
16b, 38b; Metropolitan Museum of Art,
New York, Purchase 1947, Joseph Pulitzer
Bequest P40a; National Bibliothek
Osterreichische p25b; Picturepoint p34b;
Planet Earth Pictures p45a (photograph Flip
Schulke); Scala p41a.

The publishers have made every effort to
trace the copyright holders, but if they
have inadvertently overlooked any, they
will be pleased to make the necessary
arrangement at the first opportunity.

Cover photograph © Michael Holford

Note to the reader – In this book there are some words in the text which are printed in **bold** type. This shows that the word is lited in the glossary on page 62. The glossary gives a brief explanation of words which may be new to you.

Contents

Who were the Greeks?

People today still admire the work of Greek thinkers, writers and artists who lived a very long time ago.

The Minoans

About 5000 years ago people living on the island of Crete began to build and paint and make beautiful objects. They knew how to read and write, but their language was not Greek. They were called the Minoans because their king was called King Minos.

This is a ruined Greek temple. There are lots of ruins like this. They are looked after now so that they do not collapse any further.

Greek craftsmen made beautiful jewellery like this. They used silver, gold and precious stones. This jewellery was made thousands of years ago.

The first Greeks

The first Greek-speaking people moved onto mainland Greece from about 2000BC. They came from the north and the east. They learned from the Minoans and built beautiful palaces at places like Mycenae. Gradually, in each town and surrounding countryside, people began living in small groups. These towns were called **city-states**. By 300BC Athens was the largest and most powerful city-state. Greek learning and ideas spread far and wide.

This map shows the most important Greek city-states.

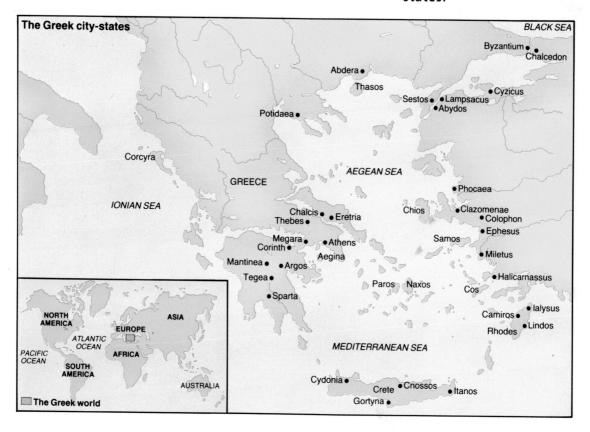

The Greek city-states

BLACK SEA
Byzantium
Chalcedon
Abdera
Thasos
Cyzicus
Sestos • Lampsacus
Abydos
Potidaea
Corcyra
AEGEAN SEA
GREECE
Phocaea
IONIAN SEA
Chalcis • Eretria
Thebes
Chios
Clazomenae
Colophon
Ephesus
Megara • Athens
Corinth
Aegina
Samos
Miletus
Mantinea • Argos
Tegea
Paros   Naxos
Cos
Halicarnassus
Sparta
Camiros • Ialysus
Rhodes • Lindos
MEDITERRANEAN SEA
Cydonia
Crete • Cnossos
Itanos
Gortyna

NORTH AMERICA
ASIA
EUROPE
ATLANTIC OCEAN
AFRICA
PACIFIC OCEAN
SOUTH AMERICA
AUSTRALIA
The Greek world

How we know about the Greeks

If you visited a museum you could look at objects or **artefacts** made and used by the Greeks. You could see artefacts such as coins and toys, statues and jewellery. Most of these artefacts were dug out of the ground by **archaeologists**. These are people who have been specially trained to **excavate** and uncover ruins of old buildings and towns. They also find everyday objects including bits of pots and tiles. Using what they find, the archaeologists build up a picture of the past.

Archaeologists at work. They are slowly uncovering evidence from the past.

Heinrich Schliemann found this gold cup at Mycenae. It was badly squashed. Archaeologists pushed it back into its proper shape.

Archaeologists have to decide where to look. They study what is already known about an area first. Sometimes they find clues in old books and maps. This is how they discovered the ruins of Mycenae. The city was destroyed 3200 years ago but people still told stories about the Mycenaeans. The Greek poet, Homer, wrote two long poems about them, called the *Iliad* and the *Odyssey.* A German businessman, Heinrich Schliemann, loved these poems. He decided to look for the lost cities they described. In 1870 he found the ruins of Troy and in 1876 he found Mycenae.

Archaeologists found this gold and silver dagger at Mycenae. The design is like the work of Minoan artists. Archaeologists think artists from Crete came to work in Mycenae.

Clues in words and pictures

Heinrich Schliemann decided where to look for Troy and Mycenae after reading Homer's poems. Archaeologists have found even older pieces of Greek writing, but not in books. In 1900 Arthur Evans began digging at Knossus. He found clay tablets with writing on them. There were two sorts of writing. These were called Linear A and Linear B.

Linear B
This clay tablet is about 3400 years old. It is like the ones found by Arthur Evans. The writing on it is called Linear B. It took Michael Ventris ten years to work out the language of Linear B. No one has yet worked out the older language, Linear A, used by the Minoans.

The alphabet we use today has many letters which come from ancient Greek letters. Can you work out which these are?

The Greek alphabet

Capital letter	Small letter	Name	Sound
A	α	alpha	a
B	β	beta	b
Γ	γ	gamma	g
Δ	δ	delta	d
E	ε	epsilon	e (as in *bed*)
Z	ζ	zeta	z
H	η	eta	e (as in *bay*)
Θ	θ	theta	th (as in *think*)
I	ι	iota	i
K	κ	kappa	k
Λ	λ	lambda	l
M	μ	mu	m
N	ν	nu	n
Ξ	ξ	xi	x
O	ο	omicron	o (as in *pot*)
Π	π	pi	p
P	ρ	rho	rh, r
Σ	σ	sigma	s
T	τ	tau	t
Y	υ	upsilon	u
Φ	φ	phi	ph
X	χ	chi	kh
Ψ	ψ	psi	ps
Ω	ω	omega	o (as in *dome*)

From about 700BC many official records were carved on stone. These tell us about Greek laws and about how places were built. We can also learn a lot about Greek life from Homer and from other writers. Plato, a thinker and **philosopher**, wrote about his own ideas and those of his teacher, Socrates. Herodotus tried to separate the facts of the Greek past from stories that were told about it.

The Greeks painted pictures of their daily life on jars, cups, vases and bowls. Greek **sculptures** and paintings show us what the ancient Greeks wore and what they looked like.

During the last century many archaeologists took the objects they found out of Greece. They are on display in museums in London, Paris and New York. Some people think they should be sent back to Greece.

The painting on this vase shows Greek farmers collecting olives. Two men use sticks to shake the fruit from the tree on to a sheet spread on the ground. A third man picks up the fruit. Olives are still picked in this way on Greek farms today.

The Greek Civilizations

3000BC	The start of the Minoan civilization on Crete	1200BC	Dorian invaders destroy the Mycenaean civilization
1600BC	The Mycenaean civilization begins on the Greek mainland	1200–800BC	The Dark Ages
		800–500BC	The Archaic Period
		500–336BC	The Classical Period
		336–146BC	The Hellenistic Period

How Greece was governed

Greece was a collection of independent city-states. Each state was ruled by a group of landowners who had as much power as a king. This is called an **aristocracy**. Sometimes an aristocracy was overthrown by a **tyrant**. Tyrants and nobles didn't obey any laws. By about 500BC some of the city-states were ruled by **oligarchies**. In an oligarchy, the government is controlled by a few rich **citizens**. Gradually a new form of government was introduced in Athens. This was called **demokratia**, which means government by the people. The English word **democracy** comes from this Greek word. In Greek democracies, all citizens had a say in how their state was governed.

The Acropolis in Athens
The acropolis was built as a fortress against invaders. Later it became a place of worship, with a temple to the city's special god.

How democracy worked in Athens

Each citizen of Athens was a member of the assembly. The assembly met once a week. Any citizen could speak at assembly meetings. A council of 500 citizens was chosen each year by drawing lots. The council decided what was to be discussed at assemblies. Council members looked after the management of the city. A lottery was used to choose the board of ten generals who were to be responsible for the protection of Athens against invaders.

Once a year, members of the assembly had the chance to throw out anyone they disapproved of. Each member scratched a name on a piece of pottery. These pieces were called ostraka. The person with the most votes against him was ostracized (sent away) for ten years. This ostraka shows the name of Aristeides.

Every year citizens of Athens took their turn at being judges, officials and council members. The judges gave their verdicts on quarrels between citizens. They used bronze discs to vote with. If most of the discs used had solid knobs, the person was judged innocent. If most of the discs had hollow knobs, the person was guilty.

What the Greeks wore

In Greece the climate was dry with warm winters and very hot summers. People wore loose clothes to keep themselves cool. Men and women wore tunics called **chitons**. Men wore short tunics for work and long ones for special occasions. Workmen wore short brown tunics. Women wore chitons which came down to their ankles. In winter they wore shawls, called **himations**, as well. Men and women wore sandals or went barefoot.

This man is dressed for a special occasion. He is wearing a cloak over his chiton.

Hairstyles and make-up

Rich women folded their hair around headbands. Sometimes they bought wigs in the latest fashion. In Athens, men visited the hairdresser as often as women did. They wanted to be fashionable, too. Men and women wore perfume. Women used chalk to whiten their faces and juice to redden their lips.

Cloth and dyes

Most Greek clothes were made from wool. In Athens it was possible to buy a lighter cloth called **linen**, which was made from flax. Rich people could afford to buy brightly coloured cloth for their clothes.

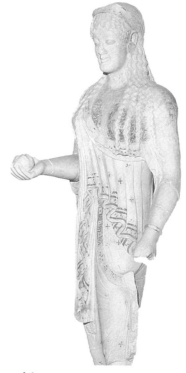

This woman is wearing a chiton. She has put a himation over it.

You can see various Greek hairstyles in this picture. All women except slaves had long hair. Some left it long and curly. Others tied or pinned it into fashionable styles.

Arranging a marriage

People felt it was their duty to get married and have children. Marriages were arranged by the fathers of the couple. The girl and boy did not have to love each other. Sometimes they did not meet until the wedding **ceremony**. All that mattered was that the wife-to-be would make a good mother. The girl's family arranged for her to give a **dowry**, which was usually a sum of money, to the boy she was to marry. Girls were usually married when they were about fifteen years old. Boys were normally older.

This is a painting of a marriage procession. Only the very richest families could afford horses. Most brides rode to their new home in a cart pulled by mules or oxen. The bride sat with her bridegroom. Friends walked behind, carrying presents.

The wedding

Weddings were held at home. The bridegroom went to the bride's house. The bride's father gave her to the bridegroom. They rode in a chariot or cart to the groom's house. His family welcomed the new bride. They knelt by the fire and said prayers. The next day the bride's family visited them for a feast and brought presents.

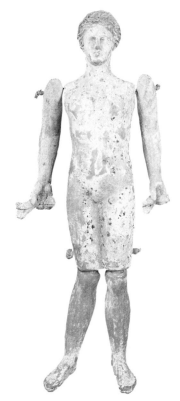

A woman's life

Women spent most of their time at home. They spent their time cooking , shopping, cleaning and looking after the children. Women in richer families had servants and slaves to help them. A husband could divorce his wife at any time, but he had to give back her dowry. He could also marry her off to someone else without her agreement. Wives could divorce their husbands, but they had to give reasons in writing.

Archaeologists have found children's toys. They have found dolls, tops, hoops, balls and kites. They have found babies' feeding bottles like this one.

How do we know?

Plutarch wrote about the lives of Greek leaders. Aristophanes and Menander wrote plays about ordinary people.

Going to school

Children stayed at home until they were six or seven years old. They were looked after by their mothers. Richer families had nurses to care for their children.

Teaching girls

Girls did not go to school. They learned to read, write and count at home, and how to play a musical instrument. They learned to run a house and they helped their mothers with household jobs.

Teaching boys

Most boys went to school when they were seven. They were taken by a slave called a **pedagogue**. Some parents could not afford to send their boys to school. They worked on the land instead.

This painting is on a vase. It shows a girl learning to read. She is reading from a scroll of papyrus. Scrolls are long sheets of paper, rolled up. Papyrus is Egyptian paper made from the papyrus reed.

Greek children learned to write on soft wax. The stylus scratched letters into the wax-coated surface of the writing tablet. Afterwards the wax could be smoothed over and the tablet was ready to use again.

The Greek philosophers

Greek philosophers had firm ideas about the way people should think and behave. They encouraged people to reason things out and to work out their own place in society.

The most famous Greek philosopher was Socrates. His pupil, Plato, and Plato's pupil Aristotle, left many writings about the philosophy of the Greeks.

Socrates, 469–399BC

At school, boys learned to read, write and count. They wrote with a pointed stick, called a **stylus**, on tablets coated with wax. They learned to count using beads on an **abacus**. When boys were fourteen they went to a **palaistra** which was a wrestling school. They learned wrestling, running, jumping and throwing the javelin and discus. This was supposed to make them strong enough to fight.

Plato, 427–347BC

Working

Many boys went to work with their fathers and grandfathers and learned a craft. These boys were **apprentices**. Some boys carried on studying with a philosopher.

Aristotle, 384–322BC

Living in Sparta

Life in Sparta was very different from life in the other Greek city-states. In Sparta, the only important thing was to be a brave soldier.

Children

Children belonged to the state. If babies were weak or ill when they were born, they were left to die. Children stayed at home with their mothers until they were seven. Then the boys were sent to boarding school. They learned to read and write, and were taught about hardship, hunger and pain.

This is a bronze statue of a Spartan warrior. It was made about 500BC.

This map shows Sparta and the rest of Greece.

The city of Sparta was built on a plain. You can see in this modern photograph that it was surrounded by mountains. These protected Sparta from invaders.

Life after school

All boys had to become soldiers when they left school. Their training made them the best soldiers in Greece. However, their life was very hard. They had to give all their time to the city-state. They could marry but were not allowed to live with their wives until they were 30 years old.

The government of Sparta

The Spartan government was an oligarchy. This meant that a few people made the important decisions. These were the 28 members of the Council of Elders. The Spartans elected two kings. One king led the army and the other king was the chief priest.

This is a statue of a girl from Sparta. Spartan women learned to jump, run, wrestle and throw the discus and javelin. Spartans wanted strong mothers for their sons. Spartan girls wore short, sleeveless tunics. Other Greeks were shocked. They thought women's clothes should cover more of their bodies.

The gods of Olympus

The Greeks believed in many gods. They had many different ideas about the gods. Homer wrote about gods who looked and behaved like humans. Hesiod explained how the god Zeus used thunder and lightning to control rival gods. Xenophanes, a philosopher, thought there was only one god, while Protagoras was not sure that gods existed at all!

Greek people said that the twelve most important gods lived on Mount Olympus in north east Greece. The Greeks told stories or **myths** about these gods.

This silver coin was made in Athens about 470BC. The owl was the symbol of the goddess Athena. The people of Athens believed Athena would protect their city of Athens.

A modern photograph of Mount Olympus
The ancient Greeks though this was where the gods lived.

The Twelve Olympian gods

Zeus: the chief of the gods. God of the sky, storms, thunder and lightning. He married other goddesses, apart from Hera.

Hera: the wife of Zeus. Goddess of marriage and childbirth.

Poseidon: Zeus's brother and god of the sea. He used his trident to cause rough seas and earthquakes.

Demeter: goddess of farming and crops from the earth, especially grain. She was sister of Zeus and Poseidon.

Apollo: the god of light, thought, poetry and music. He was a son of Zeus and Leto. People thought Apollo could tell them about the future.

Artemis: Apollo's twin sister and the goddess of hunting and wild animals.

Ares: Zeus and Hera's son, the god of war.

Aphrodite: the goddess of love and beauty. No one knew who her parents were.

Hermes: the son of Zeus and Maia. He was the messenger of the gods who took the souls of dead people to the Underworld, a place with no sun in the centre of the Earth.

Hephaistos: Zeus and Hera's crippled son. As the blacksmith god, he made thrones for all the gods and goddesses.

Athena: the goddess of wisdom and war. She protected cities and arts and crafts. Athena taught Hephaistos how to use his tools.

Hestia: the goddess of the hearth and the home. She was Zeus's eldest sister and hated quarrels. One day Zeus announced his son, **Dionysos**, the god of wine must have a seat on Olympus. Hestia gave up her place so there would not be an unlucky thirteen gods and goddesses.

Apollo, the god of music, holding a lyre

Artemis, the goddess of hunting

Athena, the goddess of war, with her helmet and spear

Temples and shrines

The Greeks spoke to their gods with prayers, gifts, songs and festivals. People prayed to the god whom they thought could help them most.

The Greeks had many gods and goddesses. They built temples for their gods and goddesses. Inside each temple there was a **shrine** with a statue of the god who was prayed to in it.

People believed that the gods liked rich and sparkling gifts. This golden bowl is decorated with a pattern of acorns and beechnuts.

A Greek temple

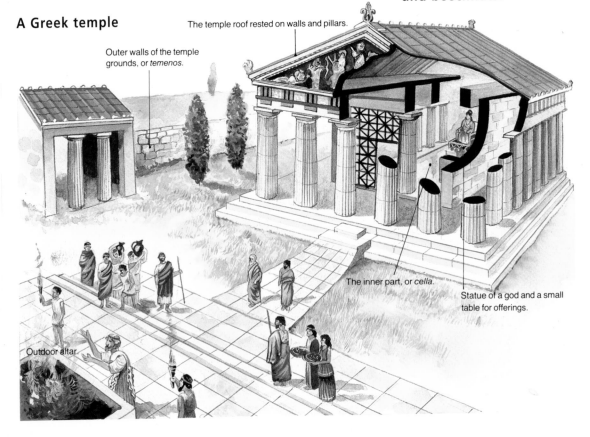

The temple roof rested on walls and pillars.

Outer walls of the temple grounds, or *temenos*.

The inner part, or *cella*.

Statue of a god and a small table for offerings.

Outdoor altar.

This is a photograph of the ruined temple of Apollo at Delphi. It was built in about 500BC. The most famous oracle in all Greece was at Delphi. The Greek writers Aeschylus, Pindar and Euripides all describe the temple. This helped the archaeologists to know what they had found when they dug it up.

Offerings to the gods

People left gifts in front of the shrine. Then they prayed at the outdoor altar. If they wanted a special favour, like a good harvest, they killed an animal as an offering. They also made offerings if they thought the gods were angry.

Oracles

People went to an **oracle** for advice. This was a shrine where the priest or priestess had special powers. People wrote questions for the god on lead tablets. The god replied through the voice of the priest or priestess.

Medicine and healing

Asclepius, the god of healing

When people were ill, they visited one of the temples of Asclepius. The priests of Asclepius tried to cure sick people. The treatments they used were a mixture of bathing, rest, fasting, simple foods, **herbs** and magic. People who got well again had their names and details of their cure carved on stone blocks in the temples.

Hippocrates

Hippocrates changed the Greeks' ideas about medicine. He said that patients should be examined to find out what was wrong. Then the doctor should decide how to treat the illness.

This stone picture was made as thanks for a cure. It shows what happened to the sick man. He went to sleep in a temple of Asclepius. He had a dream. In the dream Asclepius told him what should be done to make him better. When he woke up the man told the priest about his dream. Then the priest knew what to do, and the man was cured.

Greek surgery

Herophilus started a school of medicine in the Greek city of Alexandria. He was the first person to cut up human bodies. He wrote about what he saw. This helped him teach Greek doctors about **surgery**.

People who were ill could go to Greek hospitals for free treatment. They had to pay if a doctor visited them at home!

This is a picture carved in stone. The man is offering a huge model of a leg as thanks for a cure to his leg. Archaeologists have found a lot of carvings like this.

This is a drawing from a book written by a Greek doctor 2000 years ago. It is a picture of a herb he used to make his patients better. People have used herbs to cure illnesses for thousands of years. They are still used today.

Farms and farmers

Farming in Greece was not easy. The weather is hot and dry. There are mountains with thin soil. In the valleys, however, the soil is good. Farmers had to choose their crops carefully. They grew wheat, barley, fruit and vegetables in the valleys. Herds of goats and sheep grazed on the mountainsides. Grape vines and olive trees grew well in the poor soil.

The Greek farmers of today have the same problems as the farmers in ancient Greece. In this modern photograph you can see a hillside with thin soil in which crops will not grow. The farmer is grazing sheep on the land.

The Greek months

Gamelion	January–February
Anthesterion	February–March
Elaphebolion	March–April
Munychion	April–May
Thargelion	May–June
Skirophorion	June–July
Hecatombaion	July–August
Metageitnion	August–September
Boedromion	September–October
Ryanopsion	October–November
Maimacterion	November–December
Poseidaion	December–January

Rich farmers employed **tenant farmers** to work the land for them. The tenant farmers had slaves to work for them. So did farmers who owned small farms. If there was a bad harvest some farmers could not carry on. They became slaves.

The Greeks made pictures of everyday life to decorate their walls and floors. This is a tiled floor. It shows a man ploughing.

The Greek city

The old cities of ancient Greece had narrow streets which twisted and turned. The buildings were crowded together. They were not planned. People added streets and houses, markets and temples when they were needed. From about 500BC the Greeks began to rebuild their cities. They built streets in straight lines which crossed each other at right-angles. Buildings were put up in neat, straight lines.

This is a photograph of a **stoa** which is a covered way. The Greeks built them around their market places. This stoa is in Athens. It has been rebuilt by archaeologists.

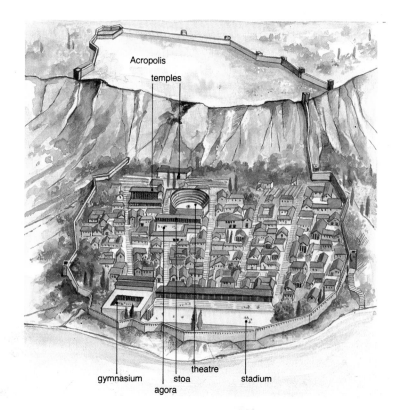

Acropolis

temples

gymnasium

stoa

theatre

agora

stadium

This is a drawing of the city of Priene. Priene was built by the Greeks. You can see how they built straight streets and planned where the buildings should go. Priene was uncovered by archaeologists.

Doric style

Ionic style

Corinthian style

The Greeks used stone columns for most of their public buildings and temples. There were three main types of columns. Between 700BC and 600BC the Greeks built Doric columns. They built Ionic columns from about 500BC, and Corinthian columns 100 years later.

Town planners designed the new cities. Hippodamus of Miletus was a town planner. He planned the rebuilding of Pireus, the port for Athens, in 450BC.

After 700BC the Greeks began to use stone instead of wood for their public buildings. They cut blocks of marble or limestone from their quarries. Then they carved the stone into shape. Columns were made by standing one block of stone on top of another. The blocks were held together by wooden pegs. In this photograph you can see, in the front, stone blocks that were used to make columns like those in the background.

A Greek home

Archaeologists found about 100 houses at Olynthos, in north Greece. The houses once belonged to rich people. They left the city after a great battle in 348BC. No one has lived there since.

The house of a rich Greek family in Olynthos probably looked like this. The rooms were built around a central courtyard. The women had their own rooms. There was a separate room for the slaves. The dining room was for the men.

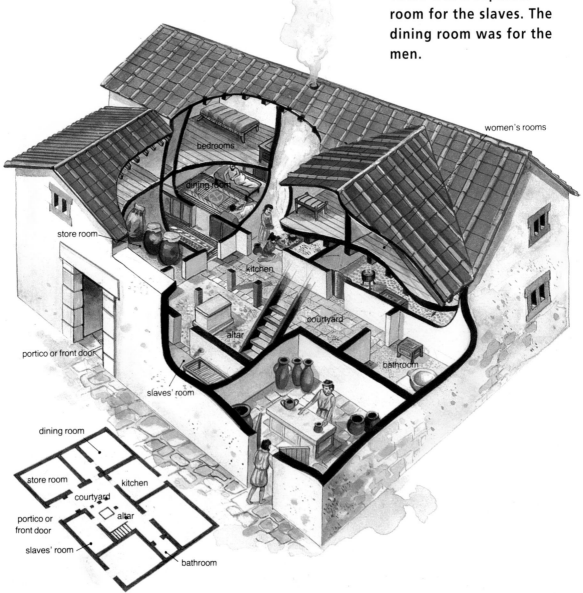

women's rooms

bedrooms

dining room

store room

kitchen

courtyard

altar

portico or front door

bathroom

slaves' room

dining room

store room

kitchen

courtyard

portico or front door

altar

slaves' room

bathroom

This wall painting shows men at a feast. They are lying on couches and have low tables in front of them. They are holding drinking bowls in their hands.

Building a house

The Greeks built their fine public buildings from stone. They built their homes from mud bricks which they dried in the sun. These bricks were cheap and easy to make, but they crumbled after some years.

Furniture and decoration

Archaeologists find many artefacts in the houses they excavate. These tell us what the houses looked like and what people did in the different rooms. Some houses at Olynthos had patterned **mosaic** floors. The rooms were lit with small olive oil lamps. They were heated with pans of hot charcoal. Some houses had baths.

This stone carving shows that the Greeks kept clothes and blankets in wooden chests. Can you see a basket, a mirror, an oil jug, a cup and a chair?

Food and fun

Cooking and eating

In many homes, work in the kitchen was done by slaves. They ground wheat or barley to make flour. They cooked food over an open fire or in an oven made from pottery. Some ovens could be taken outside. This kept the kitchen free from smoke.

The Greeks ate a lot of fish. They dried some of the fish to eat when the weather was bad and fishing was impossible. Farmers grew their own food and sold some of it to the cities. They made goats' milk cheese and ate eggs, vegetables and lots of figs. Many families kept bees and used the honey to sweeten their food. They made wine and they crushed olives to make cooking oil.

The main meal was in the evening. The Greeks often invited guests to share their food. Women only ate dinner with the men if there was a party. From about 500BC people began to eat more complicated meals. These took longer to prepare and cook. Rich families had a cook. They hired several cooks if there was going to be a feast.

This slave is collecting water from a fountain. All the water needed for cooking and washing had to be collected like this.

Archaeologists found this pottery model in a tomb. It shows a woman cooking over an open fire. She is using a fan to keep the oven at the right temperature.

Music and dancing

A feast was followed by entertainment. Sometimes there was a **symposium**, at which guests would speak on a particular subject. Xenophon, a Greek writer wrote about a symposium where there were musicians, a dancer and a **jester**. Greek musicians played two types of stringed instruments – a **lyre** and a **cithara**. They also played pipes called an **auloi**. Very few scraps of written music have been found. We can only guess how Greek music sounded.

This is a painting on a wine jar. It was made about 440BC. The woman in the middle is playing a kind of harp. Above her is a cithara. On the right, a young man is holding a lyre. On the left, a woman holds an auloi. The Greeks used music in many different ways. They had happy songs to celebrate the birth of a child. They had sad songs for death. There were working songs and love songs. There was dancing for happy and sad events.

The theatre

Every large city in Greece had a **theatre**. Greek actors performed plays in huge open-air theatres. People crowded in to watch. Important citizens such as priests and judges had the best seats. The audience stayed all day and watched several plays. They took food with them to eat in the intervals. It cost two **obols** to get in, but poor people got the money from the city-state. The plays were all about Greek gods and heroes. Everyone knew the stories. They enjoyed seeing how different writers told them. There were prizes for the best plays.

The theatres were so large that the audience could not see the actors' faces. They wore large masks to show the sort of person they were pretending to be. This is a mask from a statue of an actor.

This is the open-air theatre at Epidauros. It is still used every summer. People today can sit on the same seats and see the same plays as Greek people saw 2300 years ago.

Plays

All Greek actors were men. Women were not allowed to act in plays. There were three types of play. Tragedies were about sad and solemn subjects. Comedies made people laugh. Satires made fun of something serious. The most famous writers of tragedies were Aeschylus, Sophocles and Euripides. They wrote more than 300 plays but only 33 have survived. The best known comedy writer was Aristophanes. Eleven of his plays have survived. Plays written by these men are still performed today.

The architect Polykleitos designed the theatre at Epidauros in about 350BC. This is a modern drawing of that theatre. There was room for 14 000 people to watch plays. The **chorus** danced and sang in the area called the **orchestra**. Behind that was the stage on which the actors performed. At the back of the stage was the **skene** which was a permanent background made from stone.

The Games

Acting and drama began as a way of praising the gods. Athletic competitions began in the same way. The Greeks held contests of strength at festivals for the gods. Gradually these developed into organized games. They held competitions in running, jumping, throwing the discus and javelin, wrestling, riding and chariot racing. The Greeks held these competitions at different festivals. The Isthmian Games at Corinth were in honour of the sea-god Poseidon; the Pythian Games at Delphi were in honour of Apollo, and the Nemean Games at Nemea and the Olympic Games at Olympia were in honour of the god Zeus.

Between 1958 and 1962 archaeologists excavated the stadium at Olympia. It is 180 metres long.

This is a painting on a vase. It shows different athletic events. Athletes were always naked. There were wrestling and boxing competitions, discus and javelin throwing, running, and the long jump where men had to hold weights as they jumped. Can you see the man with jumping weights in the picture?

The Olympic Games

These Games were held every four years. Messengers went to all parts of Greece to announce the date. The Games began with a sacrifice to Zeus.

The athletes were not professionals. They were ordinary men and boys who had trained long and hard and were very fit. Any men except slaves and foreigners could take part. There were even events for children. Women, however, could only watch. The winners were given garlands of olive leaves. Their prize was the glory of winning.

The Greeks loved to watch horse racing. The main event at the Olympic Games was the chariot race. Prizes went to the owners of the horses and the chariots, not to the drivers.

Work and workmen

Most Greeks worked as farmers. In the cities, however, people had other jobs. The Greeks did not like to work for a master. They preferred to work for themselves because it made them more independent.

Craftsmen

Craftsmen·set up their own workshops to make things the townspeople needed. Carpenters made wooden furniture. Smiths used metals such as iron and bronze to make knives and armour. Basket-makers used reeds to make baskets. These were used for storing wool, fruit and grain. Potters made cups, plates, bowls and jars. All craftsmen were men. Women worked at home.

In this picture a cobbler is making a sandal. Tools for shaping and sewing shoes hang on the wall ready for him to use.

In this picture the customer is standing ready for the cobbler to draw round her feet. This is so that he can get the right shape and make sure her sandals will fit.

Slaves

Some Greeks did not have to work at all because they owned slaves. Slaves were always foreigners. They were often people who had been captured during a war and brought back to Greece. Rich families had many slaves. Even the poorer farmers had slaves to help them. Slaves had no freedom. They had to do everything their master wanted. This gave Greek men the time to go to assembly meetings and take part in the government of the city-state.

This is a painting on a vase. It shows workers heating metals in a furnace. Metal-workers made knives and cooking pots. Men who worked with bronze made buckles and helmets for the army. Silver and gold-workers made jewellery.

The agora

The **agora** was a large open space in the centre of most Greek cities. The word agora meant a meeting or assembly. Later it came to mean a market place.

The market place

The Greeks divided the agora into areas for different types of produce. The areas were called 'fish', 'wine', 'cheese' and so on. The market traders put out their goods on stalls to sell. Bankers sat at counters on the agora. They were ready to lend money to people who wanted to borrow. Markets were always very busy.

The men on this vase painting are weighing goods. They are using balance scales. Greek weights were called talents. One talent was nearly 26 kilograms.

This is a model of the agora in Athens. It shows what it might have looked like. Model-makers got their information from archaeologists.

On two sides of the agora there were workshops for potters, bronze-workers and stone-carvers. These craftsmen got plenty of customers because the market was busy. On the other two sides of the agora there were temples, law courts and the building where the assembly met. At the edge of the agora, groups of slaves waited to be hired for work or bought by new owners.

This vase painting shows a fishmonger. He is using a large knife to cut pieces of fish for a customer.

Greek coins

At first the Greeks traded by swapping goods. They did not use money until 900BC. Then they used thin rods of iron called **obelos**. A bundle of obelos was called a **drachma**. By about 650BC each city-state had its own coins. Most coins were made of silver because there was not much gold in Greece. Archaeologists have found thousands of Greek coins. Some of the pictures on them tell us what the Greeks thought their gods looked like. This coin from Dodona shows the head of Zeus.

Colonies and trade

Colonies

Between 800BC and 700BC there were so many people in Greece that there was not enough land to grow food for everyone. The city-states sent people to find other land to farm. These people settled near the sea. They planted grain and vegetables to grow food. They built new city-states. They had to be independent. They could not rely on the city-states back home. As these **colonies** became more organized, the people began to trade.

This map shows where the Greeks set up colonies. They had colonies in Italy, Sicily, North Africa and Asia Minor. The map also shows the goods they traded.

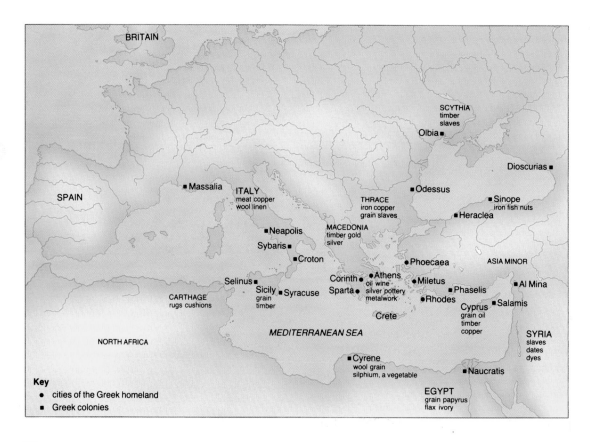

BRITAIN

SCYTHIA
timber
slaves

Olbia ∎

Dioscurias ∎

∎ Massalia

SPAIN

∎ Odessus

ITALY
meat copper
wool linen

THRACE
iron copper
grain slaves

∎ Sinope
iron fish nuts

∎ Heraclea

∎ Neapolis

MACEDONIA
timber gold
silver

Sybaris ∎

ASIA MINOR

∎ Croton

∎ Phoecaea

Corinth ∎ ∎ Athens
oil wine

∎ Miletus

∎ Al Mina

Selinus ∎

Sparta ∎ silver pottery
metalwork

∎ Phaselis

CARTHAGE
rugs cushions

Sicily ∎ Syracuse
grain
timber

∎ Rhodes

∎ Salamis

Cyprus
grain oil
timber
copper

Crete

SYRIA
slaves
dates
dyes

NORTH AFRICA

MEDITERRANEAN SEA

∎ Cyrene
wool grain
silphium, a vegetable

∎ Naucratis

Key
● cities of the Greek homeland
∎ Greek colonies

EGYPT
grain papyrus
flax ivory

Trade

If people living in the colonies had more
goods than they needed, they sent them to
Greece. They sent grain, timber and metals.
They bought goods they needed, such as
pottery, oil, silver, wool and papyrus.

Athens had a large fleet of trading ships.
Each trader had his own ship. Traders sailed
from April to September when the weather
was good. They bought and sold at different
ports. They traded with Greek colonies. They
traded with other countries round the
Mediterranean Sea, including Syria, northern
Italy and Egypt. Many of the traders were
foreigners who were not allowed to own
land in Greece.

Ships carried goods and
people between the
islands, the mainland
and other countries. The
quickest way to travel
was by sea.

Transport

The easiest way to travel was by ship. Ships kept as close to land as possible. When they had to sail across the open sea, Greek sailors steered by the sun during the day and by the stars at night. The Greeks used big wooden ships to carry goods. These **merchant ships** carried cargo to countries around the Mediterranean Sea. They were slow, and were often attacked by pirates. The Greeks guarded their cargo ships with warships called **triremes**.

This painted bowl was made in Athens in about 500BC. It shows a heavy, wide merchant ship on the left and a long narrow trireme on the right. Paintings like this show archaeologists what ancient ships looked like. Then they can put together the bits they find.

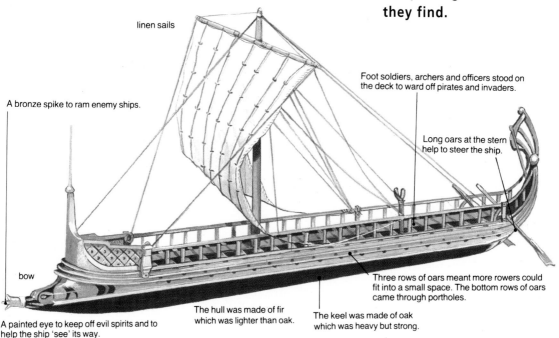

linen sails

Foot soldiers, archers and officers stood on the deck to ward off pirates and invaders.

A bronze spike to ram enemy ships.

Long oars at the stern help to steer the ship.

bow

Three rows of oars meant more rowers could fit into a small space. The bottom rows of oars came through portholes.

A painted eye to keep off evil spirits and to help the ship 'see' its way.

The hull was made of fir which was lighter than oak.

The keel was made of oak which was heavy but strong.

Archaeologists work underwater as well as on land. This archaeologist is looking at an amphora. An amphora is a large pottery storage jar. They were used on ships to carry goods such as oil, grain and wine.

Look at the picture of the jockey and the horse. It is a bronze statue made by the Greeks. Divers found the statue of the jockey in a wrecked Greek ship. Years later another diver found more bronze pieces in the same wreck. When the pieces were fitted together, archaeologists found they had the jockey's horse. So they could put the horse and the jockey together again after they had been apart for 2200 years.

When people had to travel by land they walked or they rode on horseback. Sometimes they used carts which were pulled by horses. The carts carried passengers and luggage. Goods were carried in carts, too, or in baskets on the backs of donkeys. Rich people might ride in chariots.

Greek soldiers

Each city-state had its own army. Young men trained as soldiers for two years when they left school. Then they were called up to join the army if there was a war. Only Sparta had a full-time army.

Hoplites

Ordinary foot soldiers, called **hoplites**, had to buy their own armour and weapons. A hoplite had to buy his own helmet, shield, sword, breastplate, spear and leg protectors. If a man could not afford to do this, he had to become an oarsman on a trireme.

This is a Greek helmet. It comes from Corinth. Each region had a different shaped helmet.

The painting on this bowl shows a hoplite in armour. He is wearing a short pleated tunic and a helmet. He is carrying a shield and a spear. This hoplite has bare feet, but other paintings show them wearing sandals.

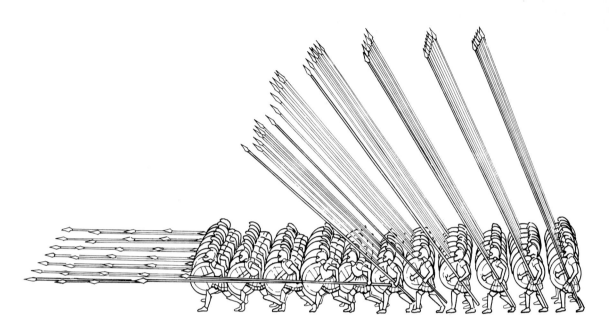

Phalanx fighting

When the hoplites fought they stood very close together so that each man's body was partly protected by his neighbour's shield. When they fought, 256 hoplites made a great square shape called a **phalanx**. Slowly the phalanx moved forward and forced the enemy soldiers apart. Then the **cavalry** moved in and forced the enemy to run away.

The first five rows of hoplites held their spears out in front of them. The spears were very long. The hoplites could hit their enemies without having to get too close. Row after row of hoplites marched towards enemy soldiers like a battering ram.

Greek armour

We know a lot about Greek armour. This is because it was made from metal. Metal lasts a long time. Hoplites wore bronze helmets and breastplates. They had bronze shields called hoplas. Their leg protectors were made from bronze. Each hoplite carried a sword which was about 70 centimetres long and a spear which was 2 to 3 metres long. The army from Thebes had spears which were 6 metres long.

War on land and at sea

City-states such as Athens and Sparta were great rivals and often fought each other. However, when a foreign army threatened Greece, the city-states asked each other for help.

The Battle of Marathon

In 490BC King Darius of Persia sent an army to attack Athens. He wanted revenge. Eight years earlier the Athenians has burned the important Persian city of Sardis.

King Cyrus the Great made Persia the biggest empire in the world. He ruled over his empire from palaces at Babylon, Persepolis and Susa. Some Greek city-states, including Lydia, were part of his empire.

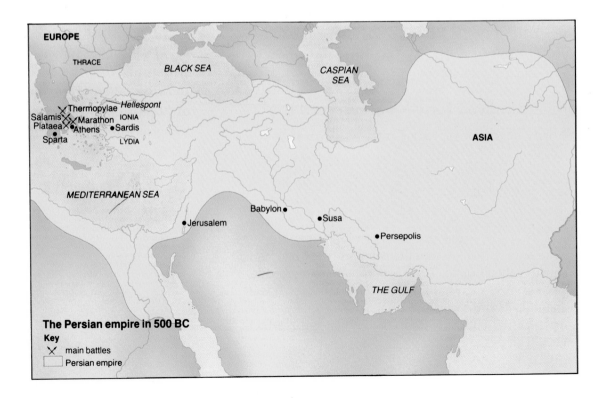

The Persian empire in 500 BC

Key

✕ main battles

Persian empire

The Athenian army, led by general Miltiades, defeated the strong Persian force at the battle of Marathon. An athlete called Pheidippedes ran 40 kilometres from Marathon to Athens with the news.

Thermopylae

Darius' son, Xerxes, was determined to defeat the Greeks. In 480BC he led a huge army into Greece. The Spartans joined the war on the side of the Athenians. The Greeks fought bravely, but they were defeated by the Persians at Thermopylae. The Persians marched on towards Athens.

This sculpture is supposed to be of Themistocles. It was made by a Roman but he copied it from a Greek sculpture which has been lost.

The Battle of Salamis

Themistocles, the Athenian commander, ordered everyone to leave Athens. The women and children went to the islands. The men joined the triremes to fight at sea. Themistocles tricked the Persian fleet so that they sailed into a narrow channel between Greece and the island of Salamis. Greek triremes were waiting for them. The Persians lost most of their ships in the battle.

The Athenian Empire

The Athenian navy defeated the Persians at Salamis in 480BC. The Spartan army defeated the Persians at the Battle of Platea in 479BC. Nevertheless the Greeks were still afraid of attacks by the Persians.

The Delian League

The Athenians said that the Greek city-states should join together in a **league**. More than 200 city-states and islands joined. It was called the Delian League because its headquarters was on the island of Delos. The city-states and islands built up the Athenian navy. They defeated the Persians at sea in 486BC.

Pericles was leader of Athens between 460BC and 430BC. He planned wonderful new buildings to make Athens the most beautiful city in the world.

This is the Parthenon in Athens. The Persians destroyed the buildings on the Acropolis hill. The Greeks built the Parthenon to thank the gods for saving the people of Athens from the Persians.

The Parthenon
The sculptor Pheidias carved marble statues and scenes of Athenian life. These were for the Parthenon. Over 500 painted statues stood around the temple. The carvings in the picture are part of the marble frieze at the top of the temple.

Athens protected the other city-states. They paid for this protection. Athens became more powerful. In 453BC the Athenians made all League members use Athenian coins. The League became an Athenian Empire.

The people of Athens now had money to spend on statues, paintings and beautiful buildings. They had time to read and write and discuss ideas.

The Peloponnesian War

Many Athenians dreamed of the day when Greece would be one state with Athens as the capital. The Athenian navy began to attack some city-states to force them to join the Athenian Empire. The smaller city-states asked Sparta to help them. Sparta and other city-states joined together in the Peloponnesian League. In 431BC they declared war on Athens.

This map shows how power was divided in the war. Sparta controlled the area called the Peloponnese in the south. Athens had supporters on the islands and in western Asia.

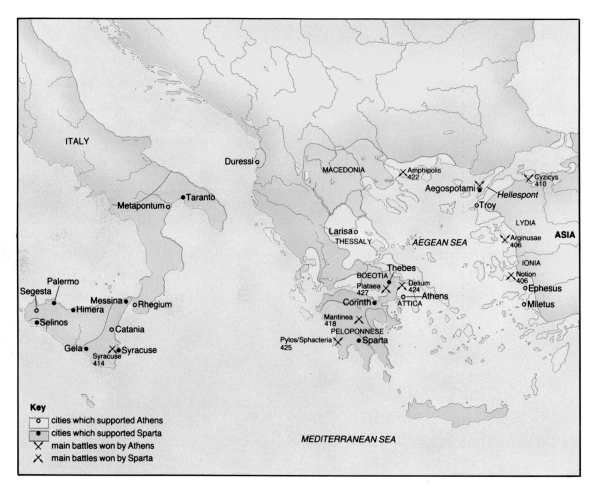

Key
- ○ cities which supported Athens
- ● cities which supported Sparta
- ✕̌ main battles won by Athens
- ✕ main battles won by Sparta

Lysander and Alcibiades

Alcibiades lived in Athens. He wanted to be rich and famous. He hoped that the war would bring him power. It was his idea to attack Sicily. Sadly for him, this was where the Athenian fleet lost their first battle. It was Lysander, the Spartan admiral, who finally defeated the Athenian fleet.

This statue is of Thucydides. He wrote a history of the Peloponnesian wars.

The Spartans and Athenians fought battle after battle. The Spartans could not capture Athens. The city walls were too strong. The Athenian navy attacked Sparta's allies from the sea. The Peloponnesian League did not have enough ships to defeat Athens' navy. Then the Spartans decided to get help from the Persians. The Persians gave them enough money to build a fleet of ships. A Spartan general, Lysander, launched a surprise attack in the harbour at Aegospotami. He defeated the Athenian fleet there. Then he sailed back to Piraeus, the port for Athens. His ships stopped food getting in to Athens. People starved. Athens surrendered.

This shows a wife saying good-bye to her husband who is going to war.

The defeat of the city-states

Sparta defeated Athens in the Peloponnesian Wars. At first the Greek city-states were glad to be free from the rule of the Athenian Empire. However, they soon realized that they were worse off than before. The Spartans tried to rule the city-states themselves. They were harsh rulers.

Philip of Macedon made Pella his capital city. He took over the gold and silver mines of his neighbours. He trained his men to be fierce soldiers and horsemen.

THRACE

MACEDONIA

Pella●

Vergina●

GREECE

AEGEAN SEA

Chaeronea✕   ●Thebes

●Athens

Key
○ gold and silver mines

Sparta●

General Epaminondas of Thebes

Fighting broke out between the city-states and Sparta. General Epaminondas of the city-state of Thebes tried out a new idea. His soldiers fought in a crescent shape. When the Spartans attacked, the Theban soldiers moved to surround them. In this way the Thebans put an end to Spartan rule.

Philip of Macedon

Macedonia was a wild mountainous area in the north of Greece. The people there were ruled by a king. In 359BC Philip II was king of Macedonia. He wanted to rule over all of Greece. In 338BC Philip's huge army defeated the Greeks at a place called Chaeronea. The Greeks had to accept Philip as their leader.

Archaeologists discovered the royal tombs of Philip and his family. They were at a place called Vergina. This head is made from ivory. It is of Philip of Macedon.

This tomb at Vergina was full of rich treasures. The archaeologists found a gold crown, a gold arrow quiver, silver cups and bowls, and bronze armour. The tomb is decorated with pictures of a lion hunt.

Alexander the Great

Alexander was a brave and brilliant leader. He loved Greek poetry and art, and was interested in science. Just like his father, Philip of Macedon, he wanted to conquer other lands.

First of all, Alexander united all the city-states of Greece. Then he turned to attack Greece's old enemy, Persia. He defeated the king of Persia, Darius III. All the lands of Persia came under the Greek rule of Alexander. Alexander treated the Persians carefully. They had once been rulers of his empire. They could revolt at any time and defeat his empire. He said that his men should marry Persian women. He set an example by marrying Roxane from Sogdiana. She was Persian.

Alexander was only 32 when he died from a fever in 323BC. He made no plans for his empire after his death. Eventually three of his generals took parts of his empire. They ruled over them as kings.

This is a picture of Alexander and Roxane, his wife.

This is a temple at Petra in Jordan. It looks Greek, because of the influence of Alexander who ruled over Jordan as part of his empire.

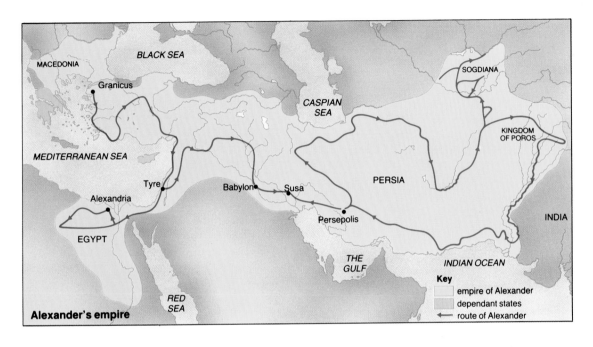

MACEDONIA
BLACK SEA
Granicus
CASPIAN SEA
SOGDIANA
MEDITERRANEAN SEA
KINGDOM OF POROS
Tyre
Babylon
Susa
PERSIA
Alexandria
Persepolis
INDIA
EGYPT
THE GULF
INDIAN OCEAN
RED SEA

Key
empire of Alexander
dependant states
route of Alexander

Alexander's empire

This is a map of Alexander's empire. Alexander and his army fought for eleven years to gain this empire. The red line shows where he and his army went.

Science in Greece 336–146bc

Many famous discoveries were made in the Greek Empire at this time.

Euclid and Pythagoras worked out the rules of geometry.

Aristarchus found out that the sun, not the earth, is the centre of our universe.

Erathsthenes worked out the distance round the earth.

Ptolemy I set up a special institute for research at Alexandria in Egypt. It was called the Mouseion. It was a place where poets, scientists and scholars could study.

The rise of Rome

The Romans built a trading centre on the river Tiber in Italy. This grew into the city of Rome. The Romans began to trade with the cities around the Mediterranean Sea. They wanted power. In 146BC they conquered Carthage in North Africa. Then they turned their attention to Greece.

The Romans gradually took over Alexander's empire. In 168BC a Roman army destroyed Macedonia. Then the Roman general Pompey defeated the King of Syria in 65BC. The Roman Emperor Augustus took over Egypt in 30BC. The Romans had become the most powerful rulers in the world.

This is a painting of philosophers in ancient Greece. It was painted in Renaissance times. It shows what the painter Raphael imagined the philosophers to have been like.

The legacy of Greece

The Romans were fascinated by Greek art, architecture and learning. They took Greek works of art to Rome. They copied Greek architecture. Young Romans went to Athens to learn from the philosophers and artists. Invaders conquered Rome in AD476. People forgot about Greek and Roman art and learning. Nearly 1000 years later some people in Italy began to read Greek philosophy. They paid archaeologists to look for Greek statues and paintings. This was the beginning of the **Renaissance**. Ancient Greek civilization has influenced people ever since.

This pot was made in about 1790. It was made at a factory in England, which belonged to Josiah Wedgwood. You can see that it is very like the pots made in ancient Greece but it is more delicate.

This is the British Museum in London. It was built in 1915. It has Ionic columns and carved decorations which are like those in ancient Greece.

59

Timeline

BC

c 2000 First Greek-speaking peoples invade Greek mainland.
Minoan civilization begins on Crete.

1600 Mycenaean civilization of Greece begins. Small, rich kingdoms flourish.

1200 The kingdoms of the Mycenaeans are threatened by the Dorians from the north.

1150 The Mycenaean kingdoms are destroyed. The Mycenaean Age ends and the Dark Ages begin.

850–600 Homer wrote his epic poems, the *Iliad* and the *Odyssey*.
The Greeks adopt a new alphabet. Some people begin to leave their Greek homeland and set up colonies in the land around the Mediterranean Sea.
The Dark Ages end and the Archaic Period begins.

776 First Olympic Games held.

600–500 During the Archaic Period many city-states are governed by oligarchies. Greek coins are first made.
By the end of this period democracy begins in Athens.

546 The Persians conquer Ionia as their empire spreads.

500 Archaic Period ends. Classical Period begins.

493 Ionian and Athenian supporters try to rebel against Persian rule, but are defeated.

490 Persians invade Greece and raid Athens. They are defeated at the Battle of Marathon.

480 Persian fleet defeated by Athenians at the Battle of Salamis.

479 Greeks defeat Persian armies at Plataea.
End of Persian invasions.

477 Delian League set up between Athens and other Greek states.

c 449 — Peace made with Persia. Athens begins to flourish under its new leader, Pericles, and the Parthenon is built.

431–404 — The Peloponnesian Wars are fought between Athens and Sparta.

404 — Athens surrenders to Sparta.
The Spartan Empire is created but the Spartans have difficulty controlling it.

371 — Spartans defeated by Theban general, Epaminondas, at the Battle of Leuktra. Sparta's power is broken for ever.

356 — Philip II becomes king of Macedonia and his son Alexander the Great is born.

350 — Philip tries to take over the city-states.

338 — Philip defeats Athenian League at Battle of Chaeronea and dominates Greece.

336 — Philip murdered.
Alexander becomes king of Macedonia.
The Classical Period ends and the Hellenistic Period begins.

334–323 — Alexander founds his empire, invading and defeating the Persian Empire.

323 — Alexander dies at Babylon and his huge empire is split by his generals. Ptolemy takes Egypt and Seleucus takes Persia.

200 — The age of Greek scientific discovery follows, based around Alexandria in Egypt.

100 — Rome gains power in Asia as the Greek civilization declines.

30 — Cleopatra, the last ruler of Ptolemy's family, loses her Egyptian kingdom to Rome.

Glossary

abacus: a frame with rows of sliding beads on wires or in grooves, which is used for counting

agora: large open space in the centre of a city, used to hold markets

apprentice: someone who works for a skilled person in return for being taught that skill

archaeologist: a person who finds out about the past by studying old buildings and objects

aristocracy: a country, or part of a country which is ruled by a small group of its richest and most powerful people

artefact: an object made by people, often used to describe things made by people in the past

auloi: a V-shaped Greek musical instrument made of two pipes which were both blown into at once. One was then played with the right hand and one with the left

cavalry: soldiers on horseback who fought outside the group of foot soldiers

ceremony: a formal ritual or occasion. The parts of a ceremony usually follow a strict pattern or order

chiton: a simple tunic or robe made from two lengths of cloth fastened together at the shoulders and belted at the waist

chorus: band of singers and dancers in Greek plays and religious ceremonies

citizen: any member of a country, or part of a country, who is allowed to take part in choosing its rulers

cithara: an ancient Greek wooden, stringed musical instrument

city-state: part of a country which includes the city at its centre and the countryside around it. Each city-state had its own ruler

civilization: to live according to a series of rules and laws. Civilizations are made up of people who live together and obey the same rules

colony: a group of people who settle away from their own country, but still consider themselves to be part of it

democracy, demokratia: a country or part of a country which is ruled by a group of people chosen by all its citizens

dowry: money or gifts given by a bride's father to a bridegroom on their marriage

drachma: handful or bundle of **obelos**

excavate: to dig up buried objects, carefully, to find information about the past

herbs: plants used in cooking and for treating illness

himation: a type of shawl, worn by the women of ancient Greece over a tunic. The himation was usually made of wool

hoplite: ordinary foot soldier in the Greek army

jester: person whose job is to amuse people, especially in the home of a rich family

league: a group of people or countries who share the same beliefs and have the same aims

linen: a type of cloth made from the woven fibres of the flax plant

lyre: simple stringed musical instrument, like a small harp

merchant ship: ship used by merchants and traders to carry goods to be bought and sold

mosaic: a design or picture made of small pieces of coloured stone, glass or clay

myth: a legend, or traditional story, which is based on fantasy rather than the truth

obelo: thin rod of iron, used as a token, in the same way as money
obol: a silver coin of ancient Greece
oligarchy: a country, or part of a country, which is governed by only a few of its people
oracle: a place where people could consult the gods, usually through a special priest or priestess who might also be known as the oracle
orchestra: the central area of a Greek **theatre** in which most of the play takes place

palaistra: school for wrestling, where boys went when they were fourteen
pedagogue: slave who took a Greek child to school
phalanx: the formation in which the **hoplites**, or foot soldiers, fought in battle
philosopher: someone who seeks the truth, a thinker

Renaissance: a new beginning. A period during the fourteenth century when people emerged from the Dark Ages and began to study the art and thinking of Classical Greece

sculpture: a work of art, which is carved or moulded rather than painted. Statues are sculptures
shrine: a place, or object, which is considered important enough to be worshipped. A shrine is often inside a temple
skene: back part of the stage in a Greek **theatre**, where actors came on and off, behind which there were dressing rooms

stoa: covered area around the outside of a market place
stylus: sharpened stick which was used for writing on wax tablets
surgery: cutting into part of a person's body to treat or remove something
symposium: a drinking party and talk held after a feast. Symposiums were often accompanied by musical entertainment

tenant farmer: a farmer who does not own the land he works. He may rent it or be employed by the owner
theatre: place where plays are performed
trireme: a Greek warship with sails and three rows of oars, one above the other
tyrant: a person who ruled a Greek city-state by seizing power

Index